THE ADVENTURES OF
Michael & Mia

STEWARDS OF THE LAND

To the farmers of Canada—thank you
for being stewards of the land!

WRITTEN BY

Edward Willett

ILLUSTRATED BY

Val Lawton

"Can we?" "Can we?"

Michael and Mia spoke at the same instant. They often did that. They were twins, after all.

Dad looked up from slicing carrots. "I don't see why not. What do you think, Sophie?"

Mom had just picked up her laptop computer from the kitchen table to make room for dinner. "Well, *we're* not going to have time to plant a garden, not with all the work we've got to do on the farm. Although…it *would* be nice to have fresh vegetables."

"Yay!" "Yay!"

They'd done it again. Michael and Mia looked at each other and laughed.

"But you have to do all the work," Dad warned. "This is our first season on the new farm. Mom and I are going to be very busy."

"We can do it," Michael said.

"I know we can," Mia added.

"Then it's a deal." Dad went back to cutting carrots. "It's spring. No time to waste. Better get started tomorrow."

The next day, Saturday, Michael and Mia leaned on a rickety wooden fence, staring at the old garden. It was a small field that sloped down from the farmyard to a line of bushes marking a little creek that trickled away to join the much larger stream winding along the edge of the farm. In the distance, their parents' herd of cattle mooed from the pasture alongside the stream.

The old couple who had owned the farm before them hadn't maintained or planted a garden for years. Dead plants poked up through drifts of leaves from the clump of trees in one corner.

Mia looked at Michael. "Can we do this?"

"Of course we can," Michael said with more confidence than he felt. "We just have to start."

The first thing, obviously, was to clean out the old plants.

"Right down to the bare soil!" Mia said. Michael agreed.

They went to the garden shed to find some hoes. On the way they passed Dad, who was heading to the tractor.

"Getting started?" he asked.

"The garden is full of dead plants and leaves," Mia said. "We're going to clean it out."

"Don't throw that stuff away!" Dad said.

"Why not?" Michael asked.

"There's a better way," Dad said. "You know, soil isn't just dirt."

"It isn't?" Mia asked.

"Good soil has lots of organic matter in it," Dad said. "Organic matter in the soil adds nutrients—plant food. So if you throw away the old plants, you're throwing away plant food."

"Should we just leave it there, then?" Michael asked. He looked back at the garden doubtfully. "I've never seen a garden with a bunch of old plants and leaves in it."

"Well, I'm going to leave it in some of my fields," Dad said. "It's called conservation tillage. Instead of cultivating everything, I leave what's left of the last crop, spread it with harrows, then plant the seeds directly into the soil. That doesn't work on gardens, but you can mulch them."

"Mulch?" Mia giggled. "That's a funny word."

Dad smiled. "It is, kind of. If you keep the organic material, you can shred it and then spread it on the ground after your seeds have sprouted. Mulch protects the plants, helps them grow, and prevents weeds from growing. Tell you what—I'll run the lawnmower over the garden to chop everything up, then you can rake it into bags and spread it on later. We can keep grass clippings from the yard, too."

Most farmers in Canada practise conservation tillage, a farming method that minimizes soil cultivation, leaving the previous year's stubble (plant material) in the fields. This practice protects the soil from wind and water erosion, conserves moisture, and builds up the organic matter.

After Dad had finished going over the garden with the mower, the twins worked hard all day. At the supper table Michael and Mia compared their hands.

"I've got blisters," Michael said woefully.

"I've got blisters on top of my blisters," Mia said.

"One word, kids," Mom said. "Gloves." She held out a bowl. "More mashed potatoes?"

The next day the twins rode into town with Mom and went into the garden supply store to buy seeds.

"What should we buy?" Michael asked Mia as they stared around at the racks of seeds and tools. Mom had taken them by the bank so they could take out some of the money they'd saved from their weekly allowance.

Mia went over to the seeds. "I like tomatoes and carrots…"

"There are peppers and radishes, and…what the heck is kohlrabi?"

"I don't know," Mia said. "Buy it and let's find out!"

Back at the house they ran into the garden with their garden tools and started putting the seeds into the ground. Out in the field they could hear Dad's tractor. He was seeding, just like them.

A bike skidded to a halt in the yard and they looked up to see their school friend Ajeet, who lived on an acreage not far away.

"Hi, guys," he said. "What's up?"

"We're planting a garden," Michael said. He was on his knees in the dirt.

Ajeet came over to the fence. "All at once?" he asked.

Mia stood up and brushed dirt from her hands. "Sure," she said. "Why not?"

"My mom gardens," Ajeet said doubtfully, "and she plants different stuff at different times."

Mia looked at Michael. "Uh-oh," she said.

"But if we're not supposed to do it all at once," Michael said, "how do we know when to plant what?"

Mia grinned. "We do what Mom and Dad do," she said. "Google!"

They all went into the kitchen. Mom was just getting up from the computer. "How's it going?" she asked.

"We need to look something up," Michael said. "May we use the computer?"

"Sure," Mom said.

Mia looked at the computer screen. "What are *those*?"

"GPS units," Mom said. "Do you know what GPS stands for?"

"Global Positioning System," Mia said proudly. "We learned that in school."

Mom smiled. "Very good! Using GPS and other technology, we're doing what's called 'precision farming.' That's where you break your fields down into smaller zones and manage each one a little differently. It helps us conserve fuel, ensures we put just the right amount of nutrients and crop protection products in just the right places, *and* it's good for the environment. It will also leave the land in better shape for whoever farms it after us."

"Like us!" "Like us!" Michael and Mia said together.

Mom laughed. "Maybe! Anyway, we use GPS units and a central computer and other sensors to help us do it. You can't treat everything you grow—or everywhere you grow it—exactly the same!" She smiled at them. "Did you know your dad and I met during a precision farming class in university?"

"I guess there's more to growing things than just shoving seeds into the dirt," Michael said. "Let's see what we can find out about precision gardening!"

Generally, not all parts of a field are the same. In precision farming, farmers carefully map their fields so they can use the right kind and amount of crop inputs (plant nutrients, crop protection products, seed) at the right time and in the right place. Technology such as computers, GPS software, and special tools help them increase their crop yields, prevent waste of resources, and reduce environmental risks.

Two hours later they were back in the garden. Some of what they had planted would be fine, but according to what they'd read, some of it wouldn't grow at all the way they had planted it.

"Our growing season is really short," Michael said, looking at the garden. "If we want to grow some of the plants we chose, we're going to have to go to a greenhouse and get seedlings, and then transplant them into the ground at just the right time. It's going to be more work than I thought."

"We'd better get started then!" Mia said.

Together they started measuring out just how far apart to plant their seeds. The trees made one part of the garden shady, and another corner was sandier and rockier than the rest. Based on what they'd read, they put scallions, lettuce and spinach in the shady part, and carrots and radishes in the sandy part.

As the weather warmed up, they were able to transplant the peppers and tomato seedlings they'd gone back to the store to buy. By then some of the other plants were starting to poke up green shoots, so they hauled out the mulch that their dad had made by running the lawnmower over the old plants in the garden. They'd been adding to it ever since with grass clippings and straw, so they had plenty to cover the garden.

M + M'S
MULCH

"We should fertilize," Michael said the last Saturday before school let out for the summer. Ajeet had come to visit. They were all looking at the garden. "Dad fertilized at the same time he planted. We're behind!"

"I saw some garden fertilizer in the shed," Mia added. "I'll go get it."

She came back with a small bag.

Ajeet looked alarmed. "Read the safety instructions!" he said. "My mom always wears gloves when she handles fertilizer."

Mia peered at the bag. "You're right," she said. "It says 'avoid skin contact.' Good thing Mom made us buy those gardening gloves! I'll get them." She went into the house and came back with gloves for each of them.

Together the three of them spread the fertilizer granules over the garden.

"Oops," Michael said as a big pile fell onto some of the tomatoes. "Oh, well. Guess they'll grow really well there!"

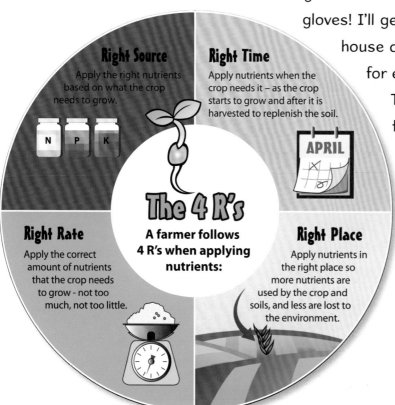

Right Source
Apply the right nutrients based on what the crop needs to grow.

N P K

Right Time
Apply nutrients when the crop needs it – as the crop starts to grow and after it is harvested to replenish the soil.

APRIL

The 4 R's
A farmer follows 4 R's when applying nutrients:

Right Rate
Apply the correct amount of nutrients that the crop needs to grow - not too much, not too little.

Right Place
Apply nutrients in the right place so more nutrients are used by the crop and soils, and less are lost to the environment.

Plant nutrients are food for plants. The most important nutrients for crops are Nitrogen (N), Phosphorous (P), and Potassium (K). Crop nutrients can come from fertilizer, animal waste (poop), plant material, and compost. The nutrients in fertilizer come from nature; nitrogen comes from the air; phosphorous comes from the fossils of ancient sea life, and potassium is a salt from evaporated oceans.

When they were done they looked at the garden again.

"I don't see how that's going to fertilize anything," Ajeet said doubtfully. "It's just sitting there."

Michael was reading the instructions on the bag again. "It says we have to water," he said. "I'll get the hose."

He came back with the hose already running.

"Watch this," he said, and blocked the end with his thumb so that the water came out in a spray. He sprayed the garden for a few minutes until everything was wet and shiny.

Then he looked at Mia and grinned. "You look like you could use some watering, too," he said.

She shrieked as he sprayed her. He chased her, but jerked to a stop and fell onto his rear end, laughing when Ajeet stepped on the hose and yanked it out of his hands. Ajeet grabbed the hose and it was Michael's turn to get soaked. Then Mia grabbed the hose and sprayed Ajeet.

They were all dripping when Mom called from the back door, "Michael! Mia! Time to get cleaned up for supper!"

"Guess I'd better go, too," Ajeet said, and ran for his bike.

Michael and Mia went inside. They dried off, changed, ate supper, and went to bed.

Some crops need extra water, which can be provided by irrigation. Irrigation systems are very efficient, and farmers monitor the equipment and the soil conditions to make sure water is not wasted.

Dad woke them up the next morning.

"Come out here," he said. He didn't sound happy.

In pajamas and bare feet they went out into the cool morning. Dad pointed at the garden. The hose they'd been playing with was still running. Overnight it had carved a narrow gully through their garden, washing away a whole row of parsley.

Dad took them down to the end of the garden. "Look at this," he said.

They'd left the bag of fertilizer, which still had quite a bit left in it the day before, down at the end of the garden where the creek trickled by on the other side of a row of low bushes. The fertilizer bag looked empty now.

"All that extra fertilizer got washed away," Dad said. "Do you think that's good for the environment?"

"No, Dad." "No, Daddy."

"Fortunately," Dad said, "the farmer who owned this land before us maintained these bushes along the creek and let native grasses grow between the garden and the creek bed, too. That will have trapped most of the fertilizer and prevented

it from getting into the water. It's called 'riparian management' and it's something I'm working really hard to keep doing well."

When farmers care for the land, they protect wildlife and wildlife habitat, too! Farmers establish grassed buffer strips around water bodies, areas which are home to many types of wildlife.

"Riparian?" Michael repeated. "Shouldn't it be called riverian?"

Dad laughed, which made them feel a little better. "Maybe! But it isn't." Off in the distance, one of their cows mooed. Dad looked that way. "I have to think about what happens with all our cow manure for the same reason. I use a remote watering system and a fence so that the cattle don't have access to the creek. Then the manure stays on the pasture, where it helps the soil just like your mulch."

"Sorry, Dad." "Sorry, Daddy."

"You only fertilize when and as much as you have to," Dad explained. "There are correct times and rates to apply nutrients. Farmers use science to determine what nutrients are needed to help plants grow. And no matter what kind of nutrient you use, you make sure the run-off isn't a problem for you or anyone else. Can you do that?"

"Yes, Dad." "Yes, Daddy."

Dad's eyes twinkled. "Okay. Better get dressed. You've got a lot of work to do."

A lot of the plants looked very healthy. A few didn't...including a couple of the tomato plants, which were yellow and wilted.

"That's where I spilled the big pile of fertilizer," Michael said unhappily. "I guess more fertilizer isn't necessarily better."

Farmers are good stewards of the land: maintaining a healthy environment while they make their living is very important to them. Farmers across Canada assess their own farm operations and prepare Environmental Farm Plans (EFPs) to improve their environmental awareness.

As the summer continued, some of the plants' leaves started to look like Swiss cheese. At supper one evening they talked to Mom and Dad about it.

"We think bugs are eating our garden," Mia said. "What should we do?"

"You're in luck. Azami Kita is an agronomist in town—I've asked her to come out tomorrow and examine our fields. We've got something eating our plants, too! She can look at your garden while she's here."

When she met her the next day, Mia liked Azami a lot. "That's a pretty name," she said.

Azami laughed. "It means 'the flower of a thistle' in Japanese," she said. "Maybe not the best name for an agronomist!"

Michael showed her the plants that were being eaten.

Azami studied the garden carefully. Then she stood, brushing the dirt from her knees. "You've got potato bugs," she said.

"Do we need to spray or something?" Michael said.

Azami shook her head. "No," she said. "Like I told your parents: yes, there are insects, but not enough to do major damage right now. Tell you what: I'll show you how to monitor them and if the number gets too high, then I'll suggest something."

"Monitor bugs?" Mia protested. "Yuck."

But, in fact, she discovered as the summer went along, she kind of enjoyed getting down on her knees with a magnifying glass and looking at bugs.

"Maybe I'll be an agronomist some day, too!" she told Michael.

Each year crops are lost to insects, diseases, and weeds. Farmers try to maximize food production and minimize negative environmental impacts. Responsible use of pesticides, crop rotation, beneficial insects, and selecting plants with disease and insect resistant traits are part of integrated pest management.

With weeding and pruning and watering and counting insects and scaring off the birds (with fluttering bits of tinfoil) and all the other things they had to do in the garden, the summer flew by.

Before they knew it, it was time to harvest their garden.

They weren't the only ones harvesting. Out in the field, Mom and Dad were taking turns driving the combine and hauling grain to the bins.

"Our crops look pretty good," Dad said to them one night at supper. "How about yours?"

Michael and Mia grinned at each other.

"Our garden is beautiful," Mia said. "I can't believe we grew all those vegetables ourselves!"

"We're proud of you," Mom said.

"There's more than we can eat, though," Michael added.

Dad laughed. "We grow more than we can eat, too," he said. "We grow it for *other* people to eat. That's what farming is all about. So here's what we'll do..."

On the second Saturday in September they all piled into the truck and drove into town to the Farmers' Market. Mom and Dad helped them set up a booth. They took boxes from the truck and set them on the table. Then they put up the sign they'd carefully lettered at home the night before. MICHAEL AND MIA'S HOMEGROWN VEGGIES, it read. NOTHING TASTES BETTER!

People drifted over and began exclaiming over the tomatoes and cabbages and parsley and carrots.

Ajeet showed up halfway through the morning. "Remember that first day when you thought you could just stuff seeds in the ground and watch them grow?" he asked.

"Thanks for your help!" Mia said. "Here, have a carrot."

Munching happily, Ajeet went off to find his mom.

MICHAEL + MIA'S HOMEGROWN VEGGIES! "NOTHING TASTES BETTER"

A man wearing a white coat with the words SHORTGRASS BISTRO in fancy red letters over the pocket came up to the table.

He took a close look at the vegetables, holding them up, turning them over. He didn't say a word.

Michael and Mia exchanged glances.

"Can we help you?" Michael asked at last.

The man looked at him and suddenly smiled. "I think I can help *you*," he said. "I'm Chef Alberich from the Shortgrass Bistro. Your vegetables are beautiful. I'd like to feature them in our Eat Local dinner next week. I'll buy all you can spare and put your names in the program."

"That's wonderful!" Mom said. "The food you grew is going to feed people in the community!"

"Just like the food we grow will feed people all over the country, and maybe even on the other side of the world!" Dad added.

"Wow!" Michael said.
"Wow!" Mia said.

Canada ships many high-quality agricultural products to countries all over the world. These countries trust the safety and quality of food produced by Canadian farmers.

A woman with a camera around her neck came up to them, smiling.

"I'm Mary Prescott from the newspaper," she said. "Chef Alberich told me he wants to feature your vegetables at the Eat Local dinner. Can I get your picture?"

Mia and Michael looked at Mom and Dad, who smiled and nodded.

The reporter took their photos. "What do you want to be when you grow up?" she asked them.

"A farmer!" "A farmer!"

They'd spoken together again.

The reporter laughed.

"It's a lot of work," Michael said.

"But it's worth it!" Mia put in.

Mom smiled at them. "Knowing that all your hard work is helping to feed people is the best feeling in the world." She smiled at Dad. "Wouldn't you say so?"

"Absolutely," Dad agreed. He ruffled Michael's and Mia's hair. "I'm proud of you both."

"Me, too," Mom said.

"We're proud of you, too," Michael and Mia said together. They looked at each other and burst out laughing.

Mom and Dad joined right in.

GLOSSARY

Agronomist: A trained specialist who uses his or her scientific knowledge to improve farmers' crop production and soil management practices.

Conservation tillage: A farming practice that disturbs the soil as little as possible and maintains ground cover throughout the year.

Crop protection product (pesticide): Any substance applied to a crop to protect it from insects, diseases, or weeds.

Fertilizer: Plant nutrients added to the soil to help plants grow.

Global Positioning System (GPS): A navigation system made up of satellites and receiving devices that determines the location of something on Earth.

Integrated Pest Management (IPM): An approach to monitoring and controlling pests that combines many strategies, including crop rotation, introducing beneficial predatory insects, and using crop protection products.

Irrigation: The watering of land by artificial means in order to help plants grow.

Kohlrabi: A vegetable that is a type of cabbage with a large, round stem.

Manure: Bodily waste from animals, sometimes used as a crop nutrient.

Mulch: A material spread over the ground in a garden to protect the plants or to help them grow, and to prevent weeds from growing.

Organic matter/material: Matter that comes from the remains of living organisms and/or their waste products.

Plant nutrient: Chemical elements that plants need to live and grow; non-mineral elements are found in the air and water, while mineral elements are found in soil, and are dissolved by water and absorbed by plant roots.

Precision farming: A technique of breaking a field into many small areas, and using specialized technology and equipment to manage each zone individually.

Riparian management: Caring for the land along the edge of a natural body of water, (river, creek, or slough) that supports the growth of moisture-loving vegetation and provides habitat for many kinds of wildlife.

Run-off: Water that flows from the surrounding land into a larger body of water such as a slough, river, or lake.

Scallion: An onion harvested before it has formed a large bulb; also known as a green onion.

Steward: Someone who uses natural resources in a responsible, sustainable way; caring for and protecting the land and environment for future generations.